Body Wars:
The Battle for Good Health

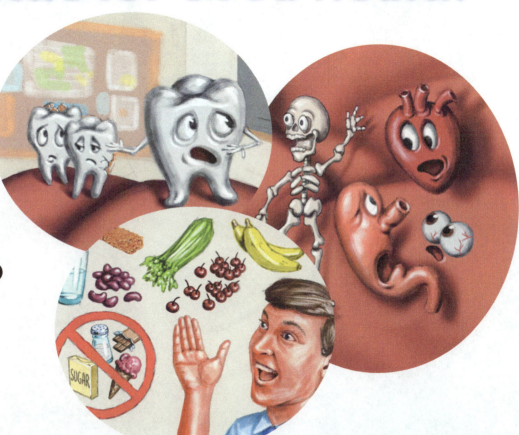

Ingrid Florencia-Kirindongo

Illustrated by
John Fraser

TEACH Services, Inc.
PUBLISHING

Copyright © 2014 Ingrid Florencia-Kirindongo-
Copyright © 2014 TEACH Services, Inc.
ISBN-13: 978-1-4796-0302-2 (Paperback)
ISBN-13: 978-1-4796-0303-9 (iPad)
ISBN-13: 978-1-4796-0304-6 (Kindle Fire)
Library of Congress Control No: 2014938666

"Class, this is Dr. James Bradley, and he is going to talk to us about health and nutrition."

"Thank you, Mrs. Thompson, for inviting me to speak to your students."

Dr. Bradley smiled at the kids as he began his presentation. "I see patients who are very sick every day at the hospital. Some people have heart problems or cancer. Others have high blood pressure, which puts a strain on their heart and can lead to a heart attack, where their heart stops beating, or a stroke, where blood stops flowing to the brain and leaves one side of their body paralyzed."

He took a breath and continued. "Some people have diabetes, and their body can't break down the sugar they eat, so they have too much in their blood. Other people have high cholesterol, which blocks their arteries and makes it hard for the blood to flow to the heart, thus straining and weakening their heart muscle. And a lot of people are overweight, which puts a strain on all of their organs because of the extra pounds they carry around."

Dr. Bradley moved to Mrs. Thompson's desk and unzipped a large blue duffel bag. He pulled out models of the major organs and other parts that make up the body and placed them on the desk. "When people get sick, they often blame someone or something for their disease. They might blame their parents for not teaching them to eat healthy. Or they might blame their job for making them stressed. But what if all of these organs started blaming each other for being sick? Let's imagine what they might say to each other in one of my patients at the hospital whom we'll call Jane."

The kids chuckled at the thought of the organs fighting with each other, but they quickly quieted down and waited for Dr. Bradley to continue.

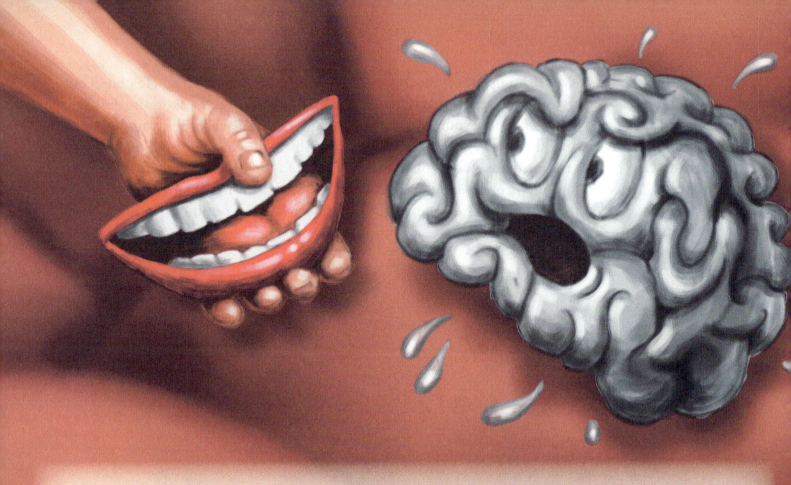

Dr. Bradley picked up the model of the mouth. "Mouth said, 'Don't blame me; I'm not the one deciding what goes into me. You should blame brain for deciding to eat junk food that clogs the arteries.'

"'Oh no, don't blame me,' brain shot back. 'Even though I think about sweets and fried foods, bones takes Jane to get unhealthy food and feeds her.'"

"'Wait a minute,' bones said, 'I have nothing to do with Jane being sick. Heart is the one craving the unhealthy, greasy, sugary foods that made Jane sick, and besides, brain told me where to go to get the food. I don't make any decision on my own; I have to wait on brain.'

"'Please don't blame me!' heart shouted back. 'I can desire anything I want, but bones is right—brain decides what fast food joint or restaurant to eat at. We should also be blaming Jane's stomach for stretching itself to make room for more food even though she's not hungry. And what about eyes who wants to eat everything she sees.'"

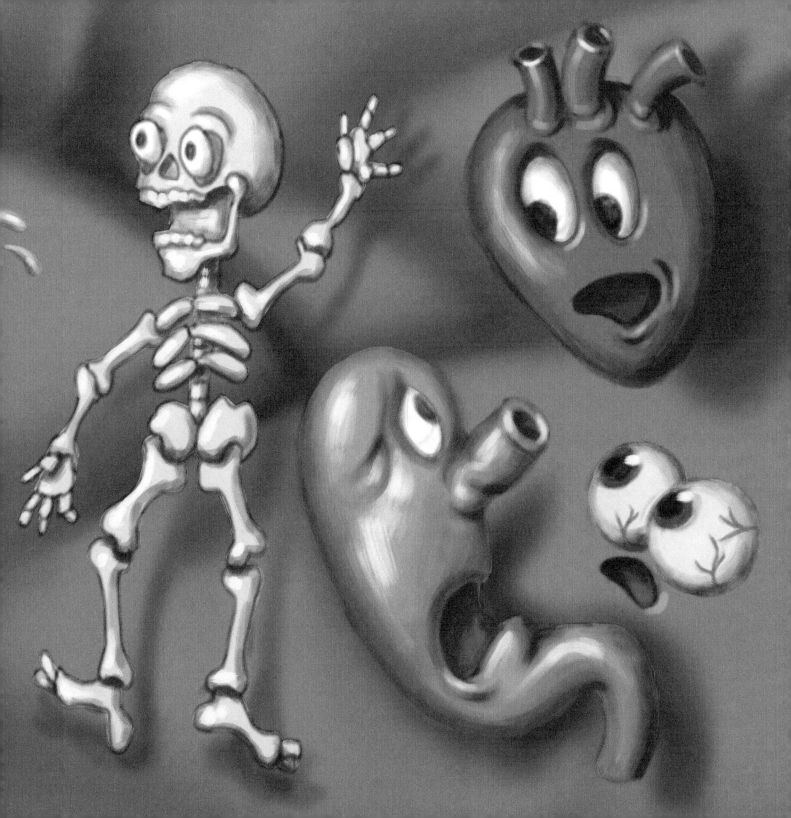

"Jane's organs sound like some brothers and sisters I know!" Mrs. Thompson said.

"Yes, they do," Dr. Bradley said. He then picked up the model of the stomach and continued his story. "Stomach jumped into the conversation, 'Hold on, I just store and digest the food that mouth chews and swallows. Sometimes teeth doesn't chew the food into small enough pieces and mouth stuffs me so much that I feel like I'm going to throw up. Brain has to do a better job of telling mouth when enough is enough!'

"'I lost some of my family members because of the unhealthy food that bones and brain bring into Jane's mouth. Some of my family members suffered from decay and had to be removed. I hate going to the dentist, but because of all the cavities that the sugary foods created, I had no choice but to visit the dentist to have them filled or pulled. The reason I push big chunks of food down into Jane's stomach is because it hurts when I chew,' teeth stated in defiance."

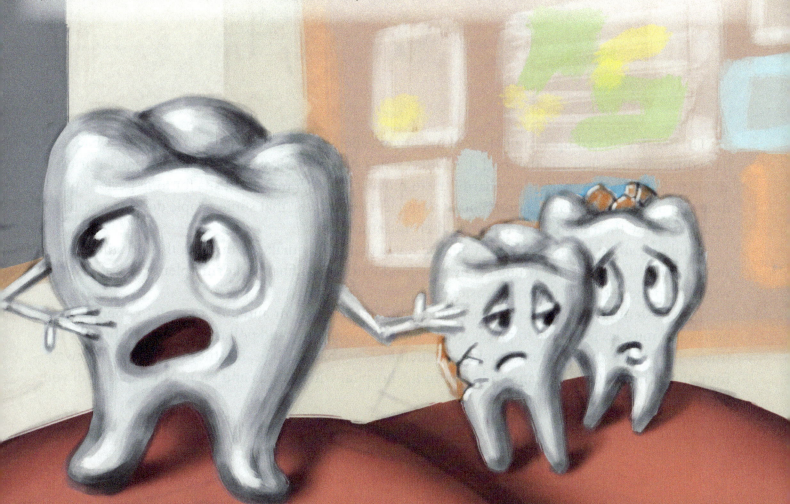

Dr. Bradley picked up a squiggly-looking organ called the intestines. "'You think that is bad. I have difficulty transporting the food that enters Jane's stomach. Most of the food has high calories and zero fiber, and no matter how hard I try to move it through me, it just sits for long periods of time and becomes hard and more difficult to move. I have heard that some people develop colon cancer because their food sits too long in their intestines.'

"'Talking about hard, I can't push out the waste that finally makes it through the intestines,' rectum said. 'If only mouth would eat healthy food with lots of fiber and drink plenty of water, it would help me get rid of the waste easier.'

"After listening to the other organs, lungs said, 'I need clean air and pure oxygen to operate, but bones and muscles take Jane to places where the air is so impure and polluted that I can't breathe at times. They know that cigarette smoke and chemicals are bad for Jane, but they don't keep her away from these things. One day Jane ended up in the hospital with asthma and bronchitis because of you, bones.'"

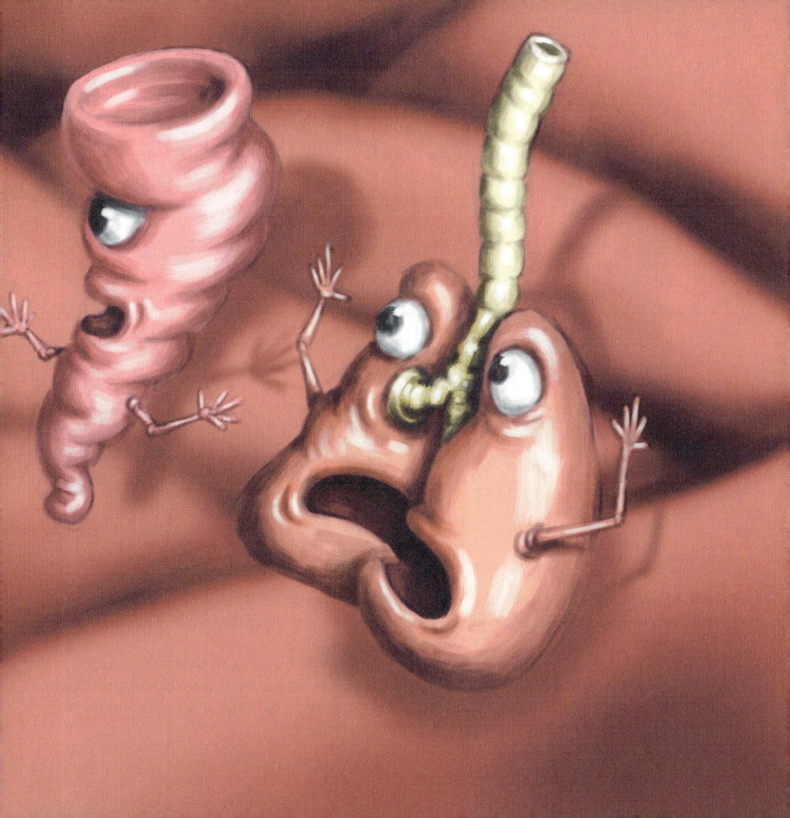

Dr. Bradley continued. "Upon hearing all of this, liver jumped in, 'If you think that's bad, I have to work overtime, day and night, trying to clean up Jane's body from all the junk and alcohol that mouth ingests.'

"'Gallbladder quickly agreed with liver. 'I have no more space to store the bile that I receive from liver. And because of that I have some stones forming in my system that are blocking my door so that I can't excrete the bile when it's needed to digest the fats in the food. This causes Jane severe pain. I'm afraid that the doctor is going to get rid of me soon.'"

"Pancreas added. 'All of that cake, candy, ice cream, and soda is killing me. I am producing insulin like crazy to move the sugar from the blood into the cells, but sometimes I run out of insulin. It has become so bad that I can't even produce insulin anymore. So now they are giving Jane injections every day to transport the sugars from her blood into the cells.'

Dr. Bradley held up two bean-shaped organs for the kids to see. "Not to be left out, the kidneys commented, 'For so many years I filtered the blood to remove wastes and produce urine from the excessive amount of alcohol, caffeinated beverages, and high sugar drinks Jane drank. She never drank enough water. Now Jane has to go to dialysis three times a week to clean her blood by removing wastes and excess water because I don't work anymore.'"

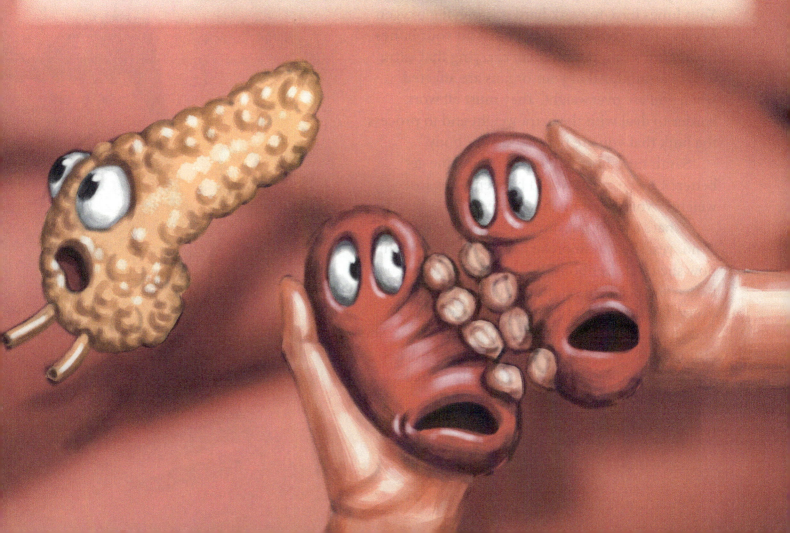

Jimmy raised his hand and waited to be called on. "Dr. Bradley, can unhealthy food really make you that sick?"

"Yes, it can. Your body wasn't made to process foods that are high in fat, sugar, and salt. When you eat unhealthy foods and you eat too much food, you gain weight, which makes your organs work harder. When you are overweight, your heart has to pump more blood throughout your body. Your lungs have to work harder supplying oxygen to carry the extra weight around. And your bones have more strain put on them carrying that extra weight around. All of your organs are affected when you are overweight. They must all work harder to deal with the extra weight and to process the junk that you are putting in your body."

Sarah raised her hand next. "Can Jane get better? I mean, what would happen if she lost weight? Would that fix the problem?"

"That's a great question!" Dr. Bradley said, "And, yes, she can improve her health by changing how she treats her body. If Jane is going to get better, she needs to eat nutritious foods, exercise every day, drink plenty of water, and go outside and enjoy the sunshine and breathe in fresh air. She also needs to get plenty of sleep and rest and, above all, trust in God for guidance and help to make good choices."

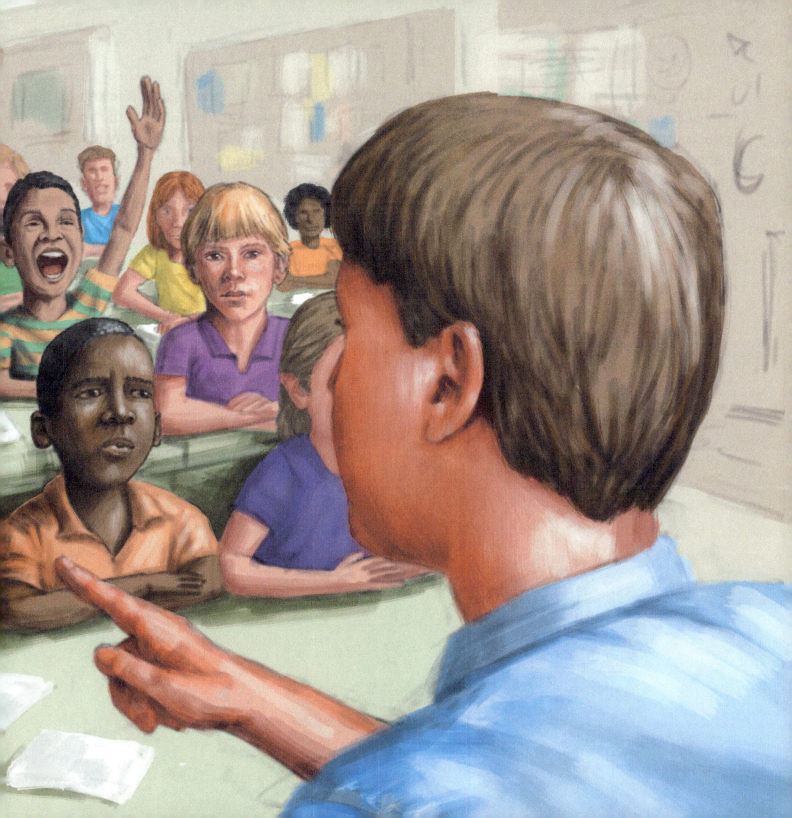

Dr. Bradley picked up the model of the brain. "When we imagined that the organs were arguing with each other, all of them were blaming the brain for their problems, and rightfully so. The brain is the control center of our body. Our brain directs everything we do and say, so in order to make a change, our brain has to direct that change. If Jane wants to make a change, she must set her mind to it and ask for God to help her. With His help, she will succeed."

Tyler raised his hand. "We learned a memory verse that says that we can do all things through Jesus, because He gives us strength and helps us."

"That's exactly right. Philippians 4:13 is a wonderful verse to memorize," Dr. Bradley said. "God created us in His image. When we spend time with Him by reading the Bible, praying, and filling our minds with good things, we will also desire to fill our bodies with good things."

"The first thing Jane needs to do is eat nutritious foods. She needs to eat plenty of fruits, vegetables, grains, beans, and nuts. Jane needs to avoid foods high in fat, sugar, and salt. And she needs to stop snacking between meals. In addition to being careful as to what she eats, Jane needs to eat her meals at a regular time each day. It is also best to eat a big breakfast, a moderate lunch, and a small supper. Eating a large breakfast will give you the most energy for your day, and eating a light supper will allow your body to not work so hard close to bedtime."

"Moving on to the next thing, what should Jane drink?" Dr. Bradley asked.

"Water!" the class yelled.

"You're right! Pure water is always the best choice. Fresh fruit juices are also good for you. You don't want to drink soda, bottled juice, caffeinated beverages, or alcohol. Jane's kidneys will work much better if they get plenty of water."

Dr. Bradley continued, "Although the brain is the control center, without the heart pumping, your body can't function. Your cells cannot function without a continuous supply of oxygen and nutrients, which is a joint effort between your lungs and your heart, which pumps oxygen-rich blood throughout your body. Your heart is a muscle, and when you exercise, you strengthen it.

"There are lots of different things you can do to exercise, but the most important thing to remember is to get moving. Walk, run, go biking, play soccer or basketball, jump on a trampoline, or swim. Do something you enjoy. And if you can exercise outside, that's even better because you'll benefit from the sunshine and fresh air. Your lungs will also benefit from exercising and breathing deeply.

"The last thing we need to talk about is rest. Children should get eight to ten hours of sleep each night. In addition to the rest that God gives us each night, He also created a weekly day of rest—the Sabbath. The fourth commandment talks about the Sabbath and how God created it as a day of rest from our work and as a special day to spend time with Him. The Sabbath is a wonderful day to worship with other believers, spend time with family and friends, help someone in need, and enjoy God's creation by being out in nature."

Dr. Bradley picked up his Bible. "The last thing I want you to remember, which is something I tell patients such as Jane, is that we must trust in God when we want to make any type of change in our lives. King David wrote Psalm 139:14, which says, 'I will praise You, for I am fearfully and wonderfully made; marvelous are Your works, and that my soul knows very well.'"

He continued. "The Creator who made us and knows how our bodies work can help us make wise choices to eat nutritious foods, such as fruits, grains, nuts, and vegetables; drink plenty of water; exercise and enjoy the sunshine and fresh air; get enough rest; always trust God; spend time with Jesus every day; and keep the Ten Commandments, which can be summed up as follows:

1. Love God with all your heart;
2. Worship only God and not idols;
3. Always say God's name with love and respect;
4. Remember God's seventh-day Sabbath and keep it holy;
5. Love and respect your mom and dad;
6. Do not kill;
7. Be faithful to your husband/wife;
8. Do not steal;
9. Do not lie; and
10. Do not covet."

"Thank you, Dr. Bradley, for visiting our class and teaching us about good health," Mrs. Thompson said. "As Paul told the church members at Corinth, 'Whether you eat or drink, or whatever you do, do all to the glory of God.' Let's make sure we are glorifying God by staying healthy and active."

We invite you to view the complete
selection of titles we publish at:

www.TEACHServices.com

Scan with your mobile
device to go directly
to our website.

Please write or e-mail us your praises, reactions, or
thoughts about this or any other book we publish at:

TEACH Services, Inc.
P U B L I S H I N G
www.TEACHServices.com ● (800) 367-1844

P.O. Box 954
Ringgold, GA 30736

info@TEACHServices.com

TEACH Services, Inc., titles may be purchased in bulk for
educational, business, fund-raising, or sales promotional use.
For information, please e-mail:

BulkSales@TEACHServices.com

Finally, if you are interested in seeing
your own book in print, please contact us at

publishing@TEACHServices.com

We would be happy to review your manuscript for free.

CPSIA information can be obtained at www.ICGtesting.com
Printed in the USA
LVOW02s2023030714

392832LV00001B/2/P